Piano • Vocal • Guitar

CHART HITS
OF 2023-2024

ISBN 979-835012043-1

HAL•LEONARD®

Visit Hal Leonard Online at **www.halleonard.com**

Explore the entire family of Hal Leonard products and resources

 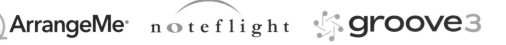

World headquarters, contact:
Hal Leonard
7777 West Bluemound Road
Milwaukee, WI 53213
Email: info@halleonard.com

In Europe, contact:
Hal Leonard Europe Limited
Dettingen Way
Bury St Edmunds, Suffolk, IP33 3YB
Email: info@halleonardeurope.com

In Australia, contact:
Hal Leonard Australia Pty. Ltd.
4 Lentara Court
Cheltenham, Victoria, 3192 Australia
Email: info@halleonard.com.au

CONTENTS

CAN'T CATCH ME NOW

from THE HUNGER GAMES: THE BALLAD OF SONGBIRDS & SNAKES

Words and Music by OLIVIA RODRIGO
and DANIEL NIGRO

Acoustic Ballad, a feeling of 2

There's blood on the side of the moun-tain. There's
snow fall-ing o-ver the cit-y. You

writ-ing all o-ver the wall. Shad-ows of us are still
thought that it would wash a-way the bit-ter taste of my

danc-ing in ev-'ry room and ev-'ry hall. There's
fu-ry and all of the mess-es you

made. Yeah, you think _ that you got _ a -

way. But I'm in the trees, _ I'm in _____ the breeze, _ my

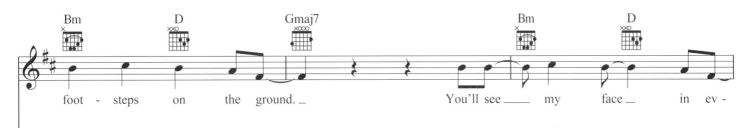

foot - steps on the ground. _ You'll see _____ my face _ in ev -

- 'ry place, _ but you _____ can't catch me now. ___ Through _

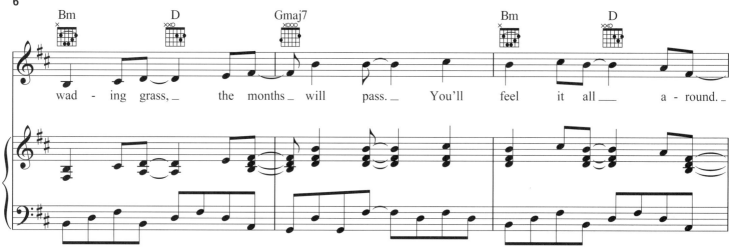

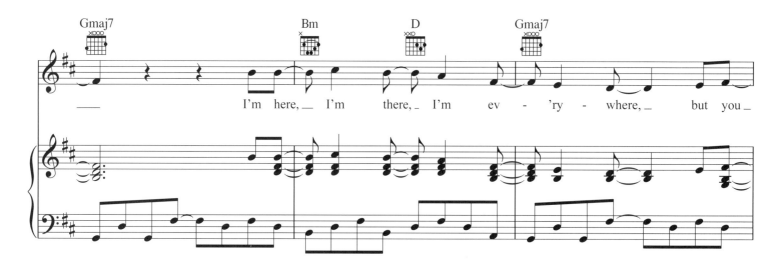

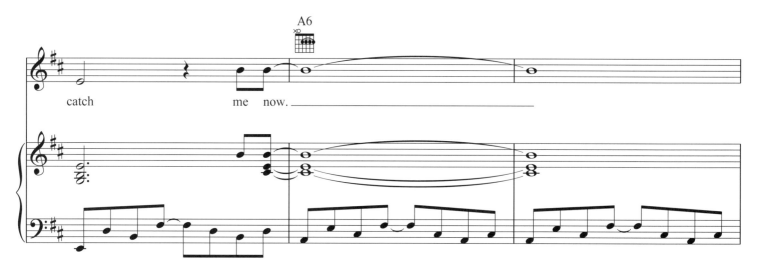

Bet you __ thought I'd nev - er do it, __ thought I'd __ go o - ver __ my

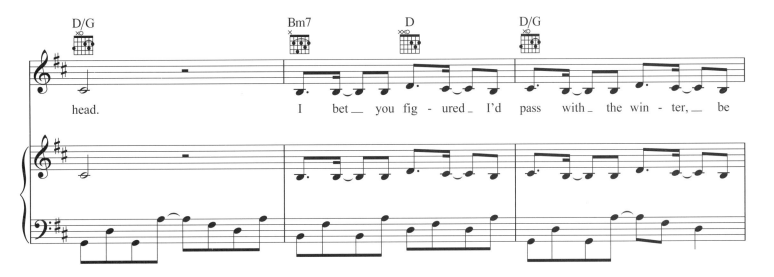

head. __ I bet __ you fig - ured __ I'd pass with __ the win - ter, __ be

some - thing __ eas - y to __ for - get. Oh, __

D.S. al Coda

you think __ I'm gone 'cause __ I _____ left. But I'm

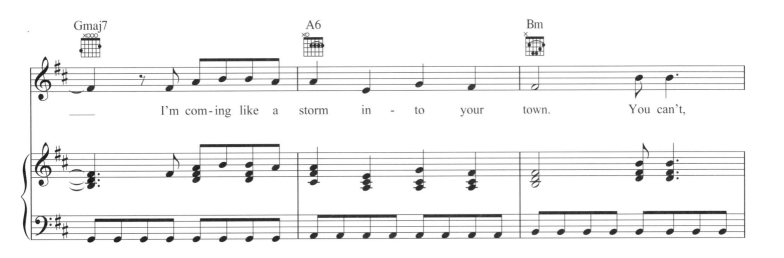

you can't catch me now. ___ I'm high - er than the hopes that you brought

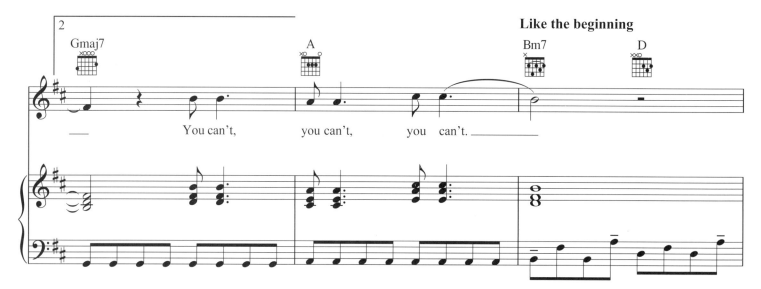

Like the beginning

___ You can't, you can't, you can't. _____

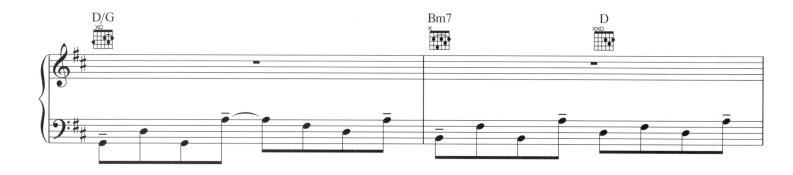

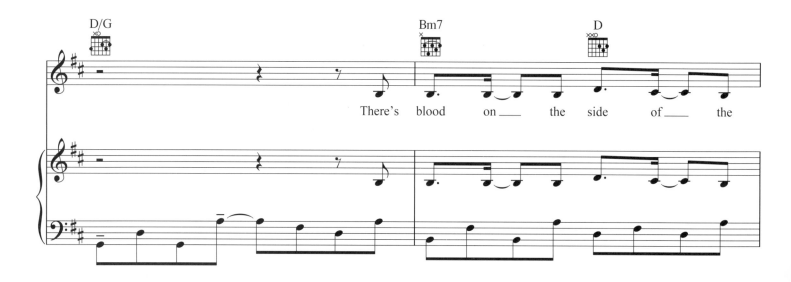

There's blood on ___ the side of ___ the

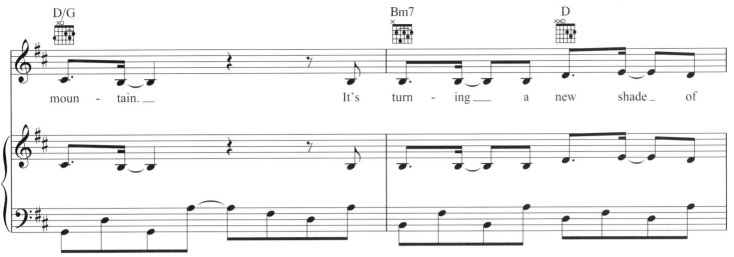

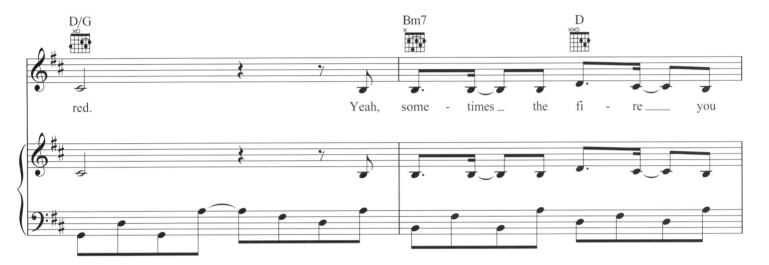

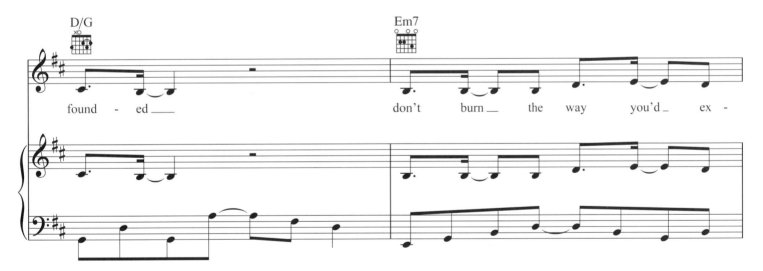

CRUEL SUMMER

Words and Music by TAYLOR SWIFT,
JACK ANTONOFF and ANNIE CLARK

Moderate groove

Vocal line written one octave higher than sung.

dice, an-gels roll their eyes. What does-n't kill __ me makes me want you more. __ And it's
dice, an-gels roll their eyes, and if I bleed, _ you'll be the last to know. __ Oh, it's

new, __ the shape _ of your bod-y. It's blue, __ the feel - ing I've got. And it's

ooh, _____ whoa, ___ oh, it's a cruel _____ sum - mer. It's

cool, __ that's _ what I tell 'em. No rules ___ in break - a - ble heav-en. But

Vocal line written at pitch.

ooh, _____ whoa, __ oh, it's a cruel _____ sum - mer with you. _

__ cruel _____ sum - mer with you. _

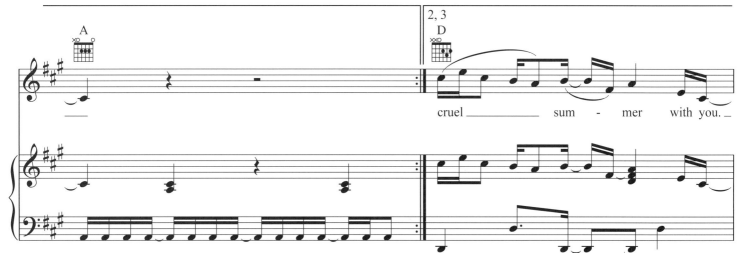

__ I'm drunk in the back of the car, _ and I cried like a ba - by com - ing home from the bar. _ (Oh.)

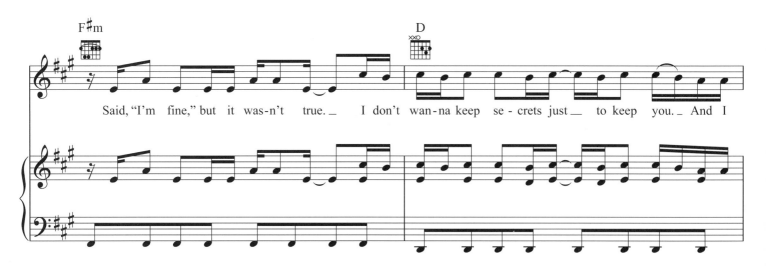

Said, "I'm fine," but it was-n't true. _ I don't wan-na keep se - crets just _ to keep you. _ And I

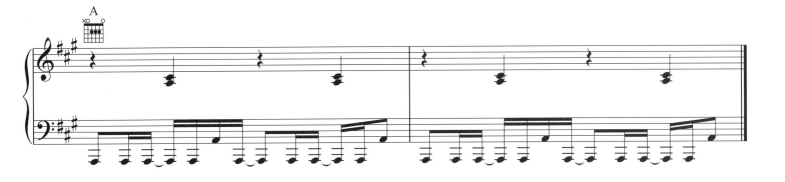

LOOK FOR THE LIGHT
from ONLY MURDERS IN THE BUILDING

Words and Music by SARA BAREILLES,
BENJ PASEK and JUSTIN PAUL

Tenderly, with rubato

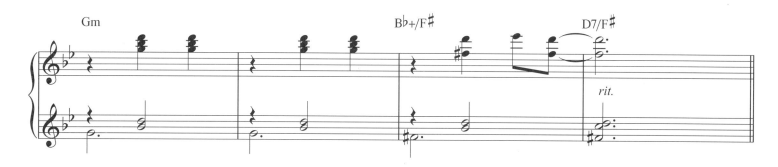

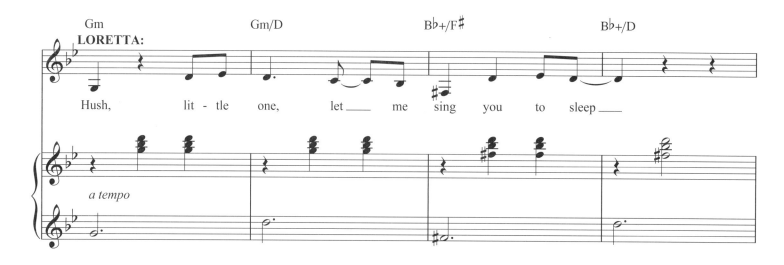

LORETTA:
Hush, lit-tle one, let me sing you to sleep

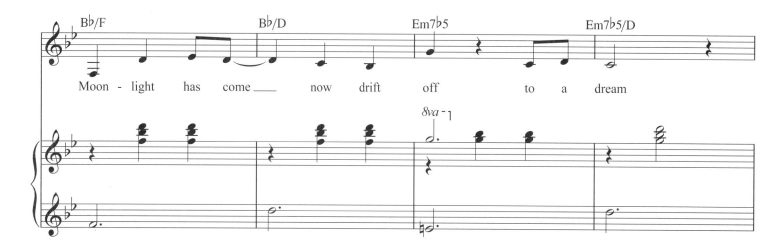

Moon-light has come now drift off to a dream

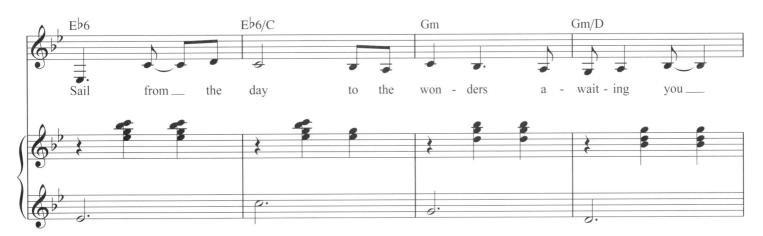

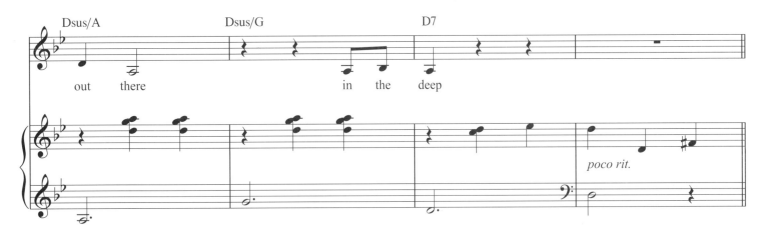

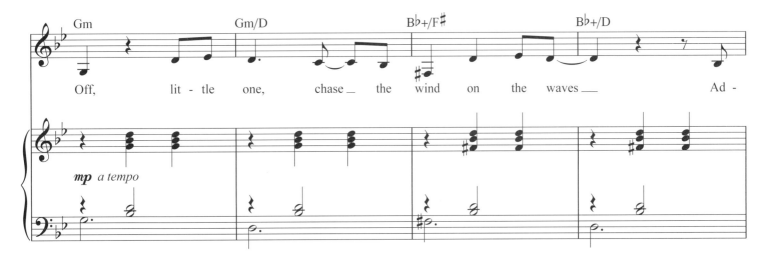

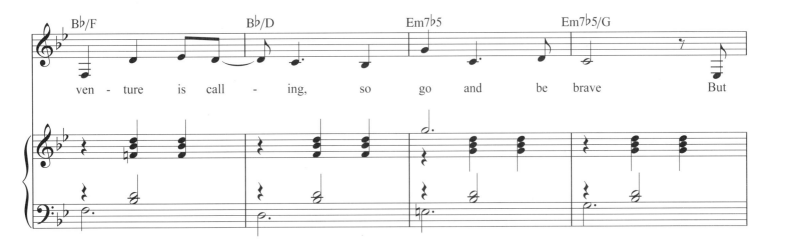

18

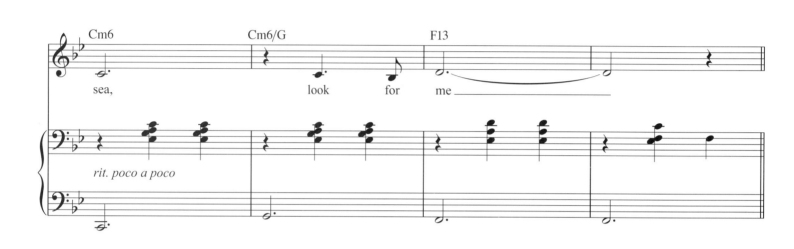

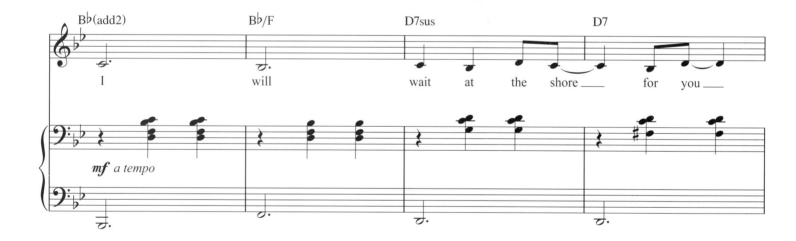

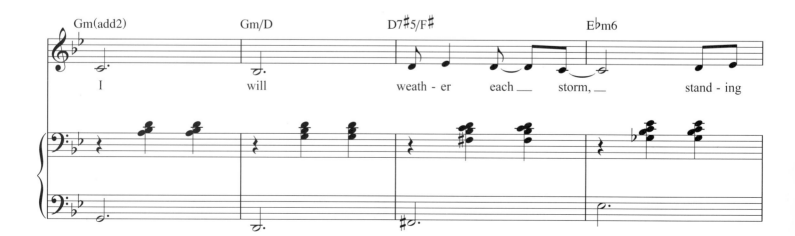

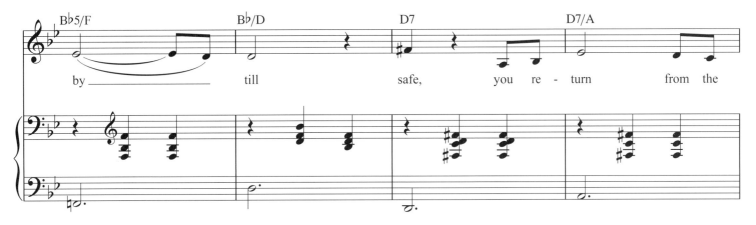

by _____ till safe, you re-turn from the

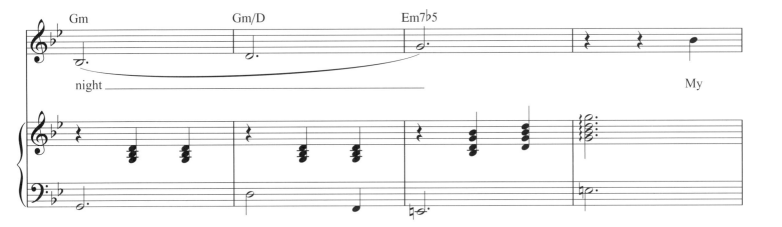

night _____ My

Slower

love is a light-house _____ So

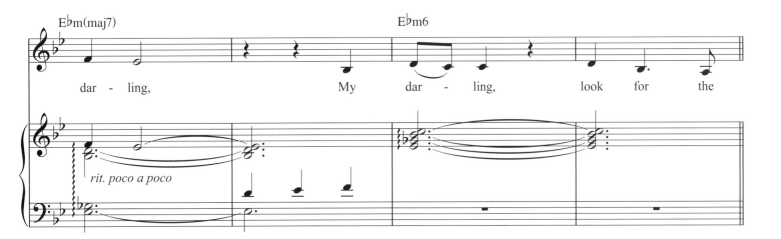

dar - ling, My dar - ling, look for the

rit. poco a poco

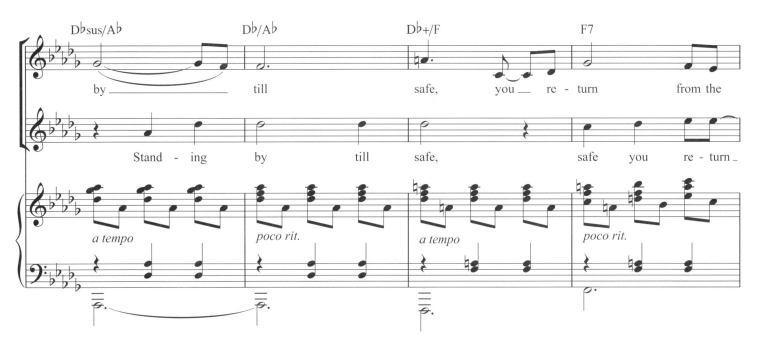

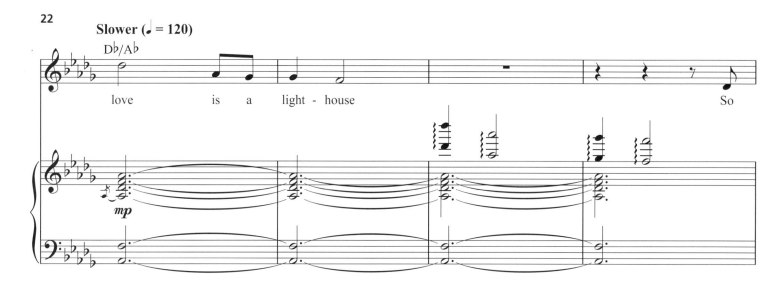

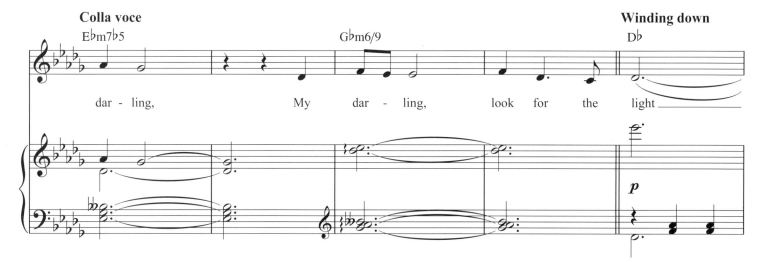

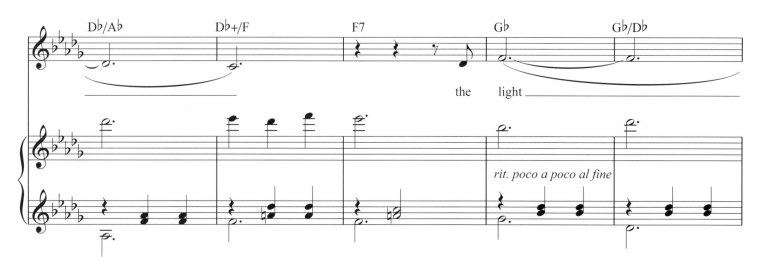

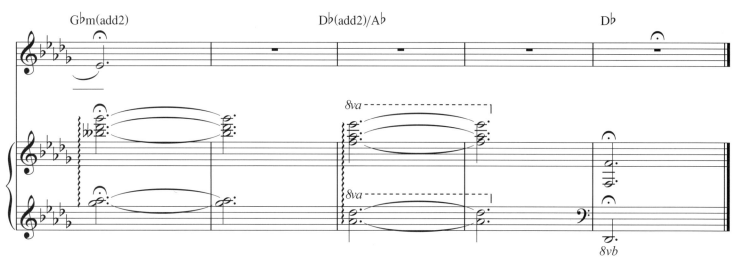

DANCE THE NIGHT

from BARBIE

Words and Music by DUA LIPA,
CAROLINE AILIN, ANDREW WYATT
and MARK RONSON

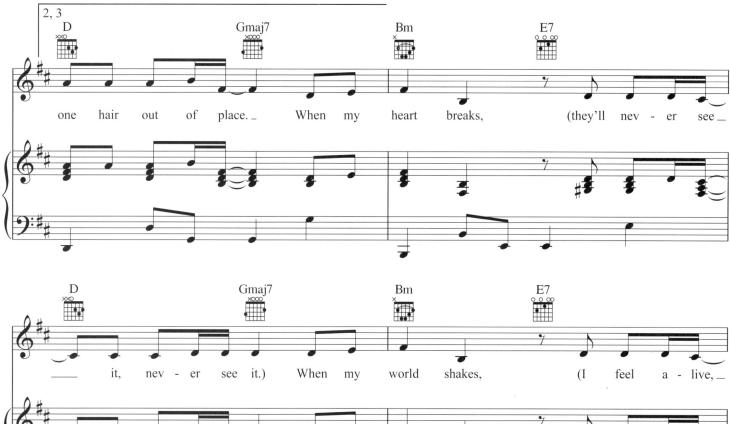

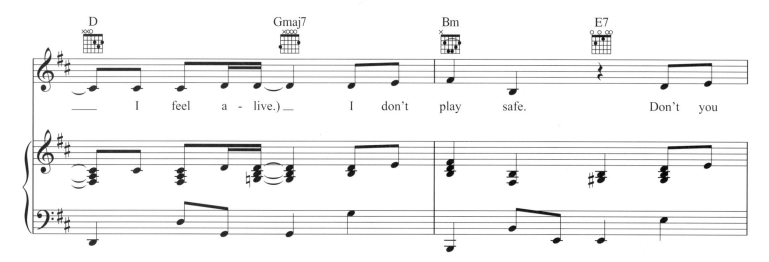

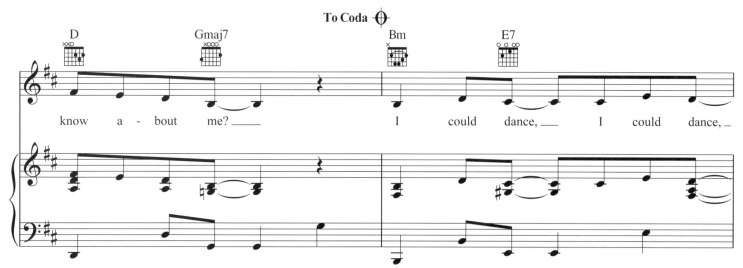

I could dance. ___ E - ven when the tears ___ are flow - ing, they're

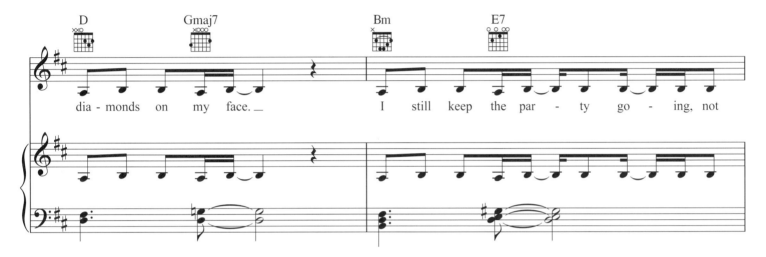

dia - monds on my face. ___ I still keep the par - ty go - ing, not

one hair out of place. ___ one hair out of place. Watch me

D.S. al Coda
(take 2nd ending)

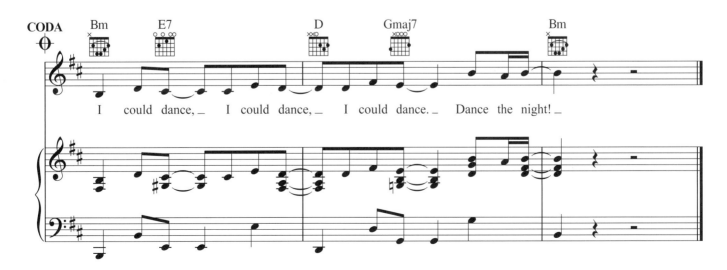

I could dance, ___ I could dance, ___ I could dance. ___ Dance the night! ___

FOR A MOMENT

from WONKA

Words and Music by
NEIL HANNON

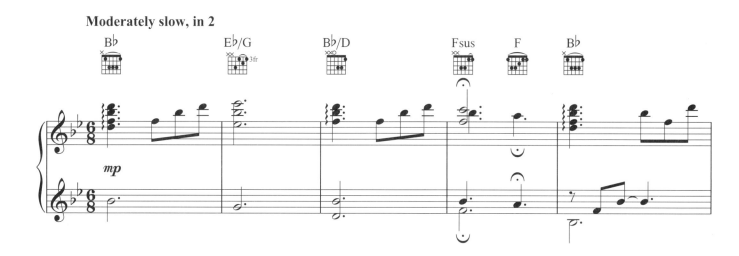

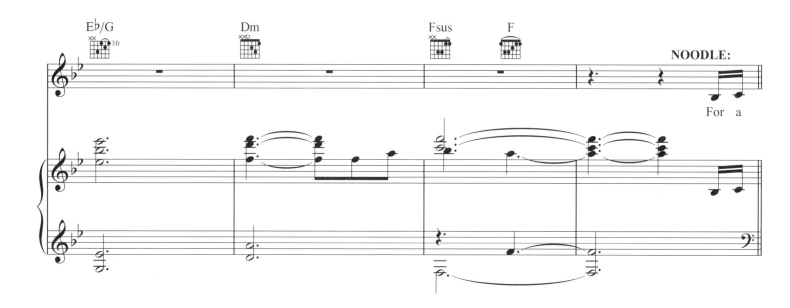

We're hav - ing oo - dles and oo - dles of fun.

ev - er hap-pened to me.

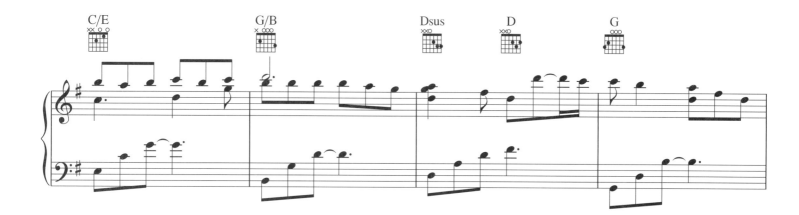

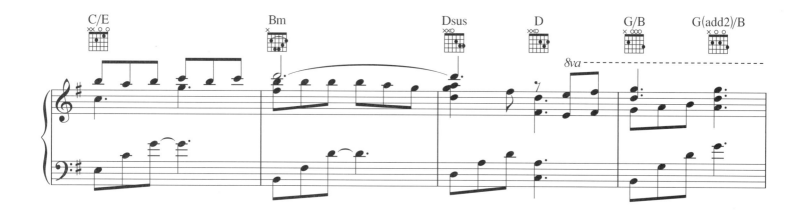

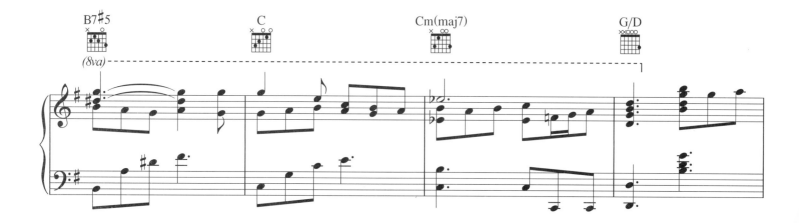

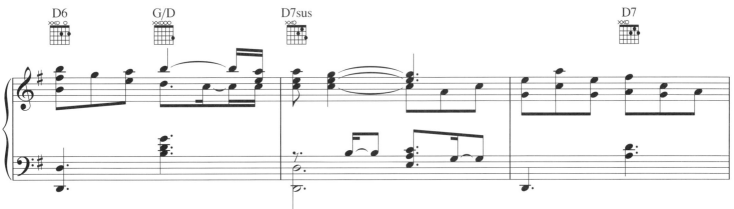

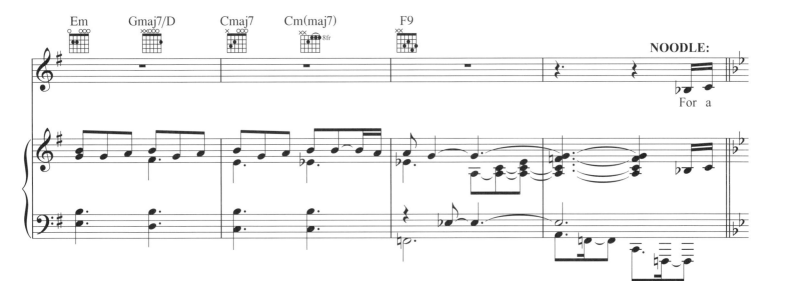

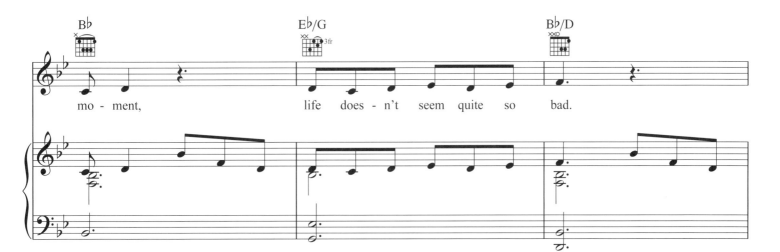

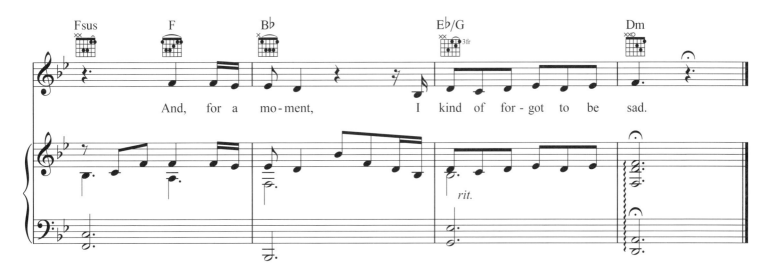

LOGICAL

Words and Music by OLIVIA RODRIGO,
DANIEL NIGRO and JULIA MICHAELS

Moderate Ballad

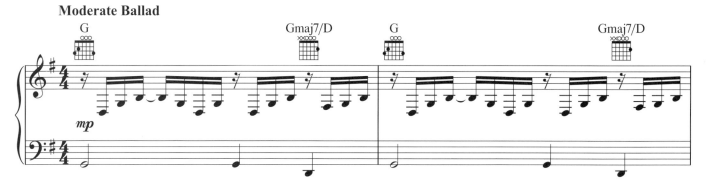

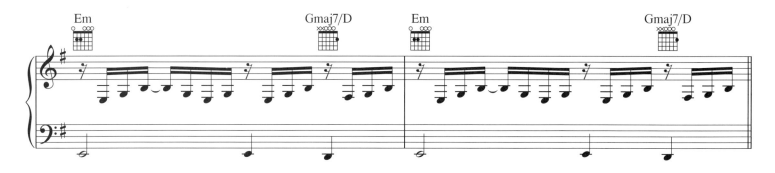

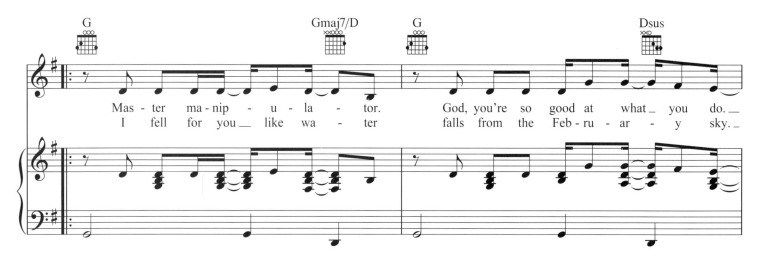

Master manip-u-la-tor. God, you're so good at what you do.
I fell for you like wa-ter falls from the Feb-ru-ar-y sky.

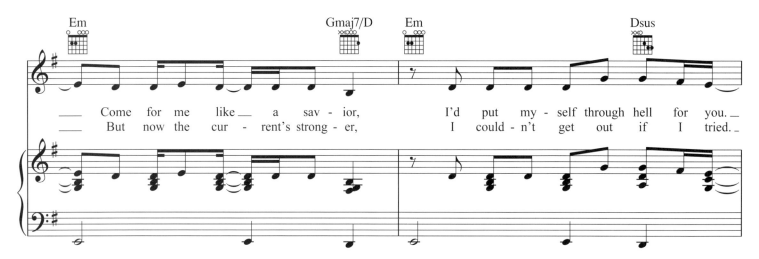

Come for me like a sav-ior, I'd put my-self through hell for you.
But now the cur-rent's strong-er, I could-n't get out if I tried.

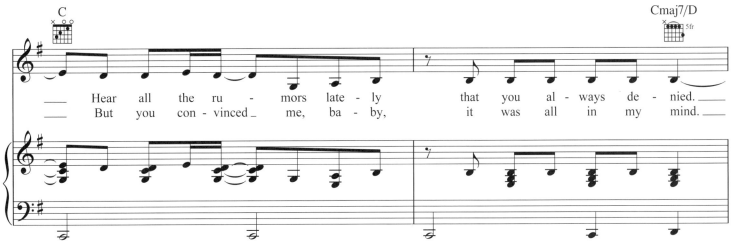

Hear all the ru - mors late - ly that you al - ways de - nied. ___
But you con - vinced ___ me, ba - by, it was all in my mind. ___

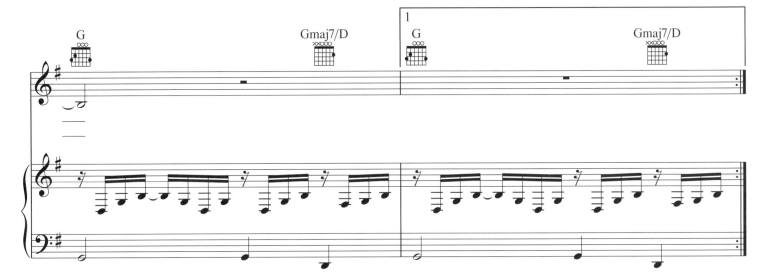

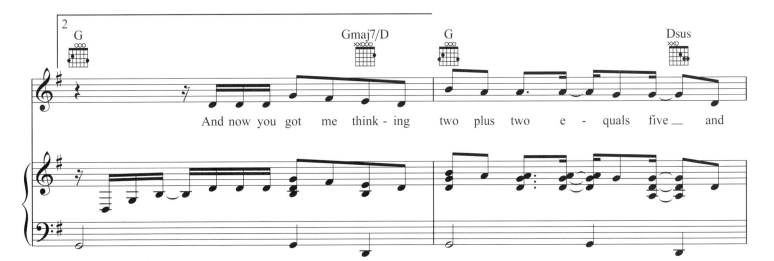

And now you got me think - ing two plus two e - quals five ___ and

I'm the love of ___ your life. ___ 'Cause if rain don't pour and sun ___ don't shine, ___ then

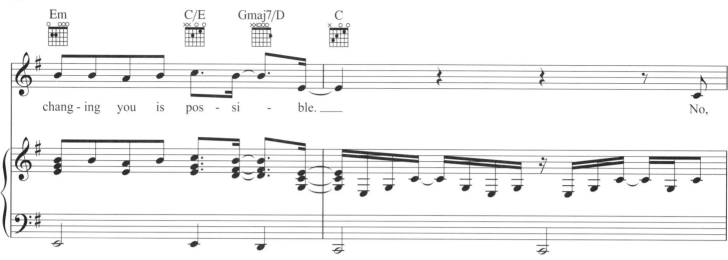

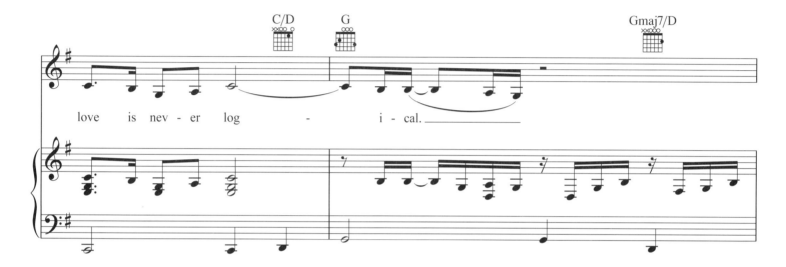

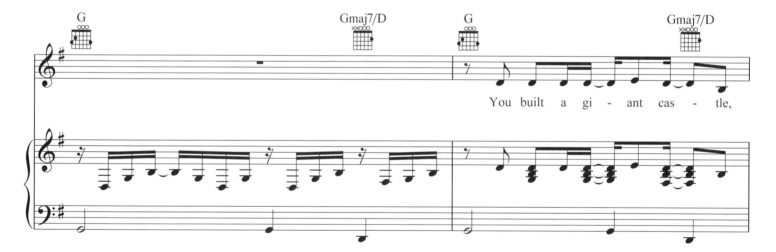

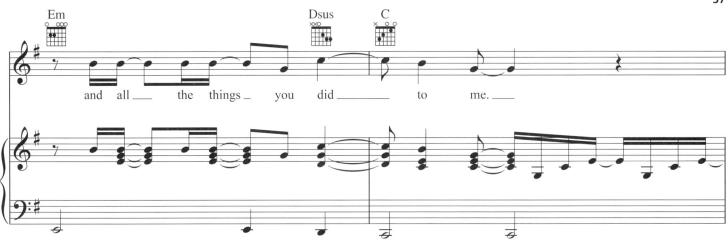

and all___ the things___ you did _____ to me. ___

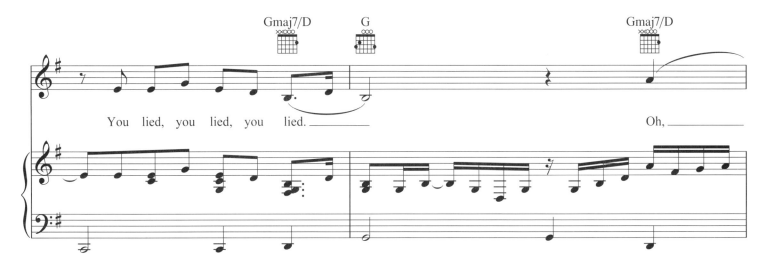

You lied, you lied, you lied. _____ Oh, _____

___ and now you got me think - ing two plus two e - quals five ___ and

I'm the love of___ your life.___ 'Cause if rain don't pour and sun___ don't shine,___ then

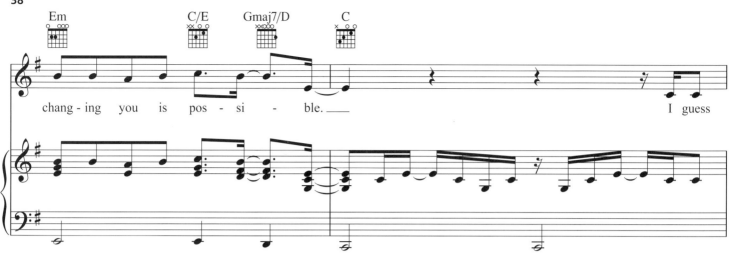

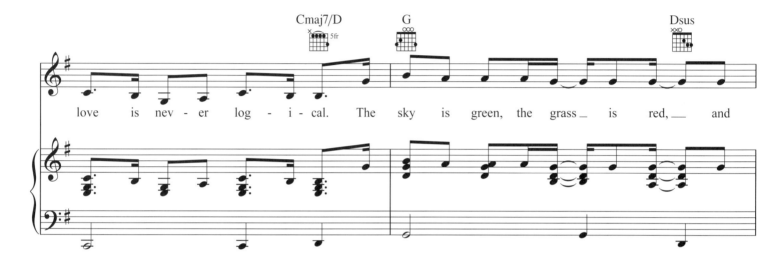

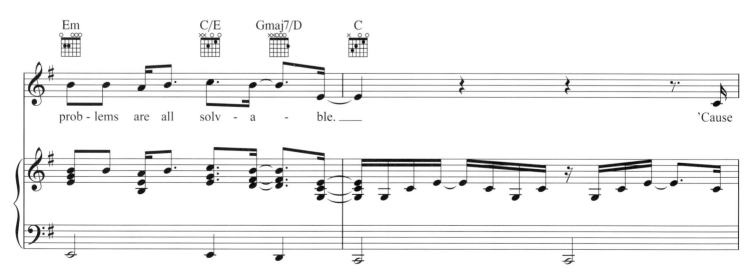

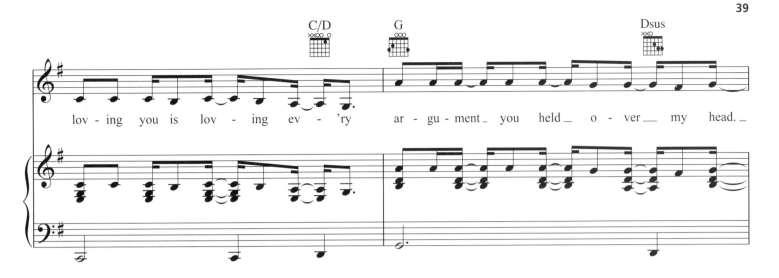

lov - ing you is lov - ing ev - 'ry ar - gu - ment _ you held _ o - ver _ my head. _

_ Brought up the girls _ you could have _ in - stead. _ Said I was too young, I was _ too soft, _

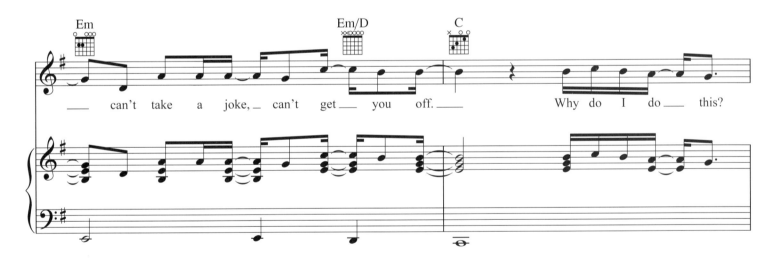

_ can't take a joke, _ can't get _ you off. _ Why do I do _ this?

I look so stu - pid think - ing two plus two e - quals five _ and

I'm the love of ___ your life. ___ 'Cause if rain don't pour and sun ___ don't shine, ___ then

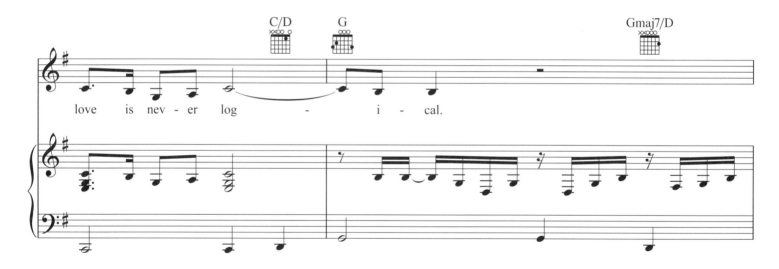

chang - ing you is pos - si - ble. ___ No,

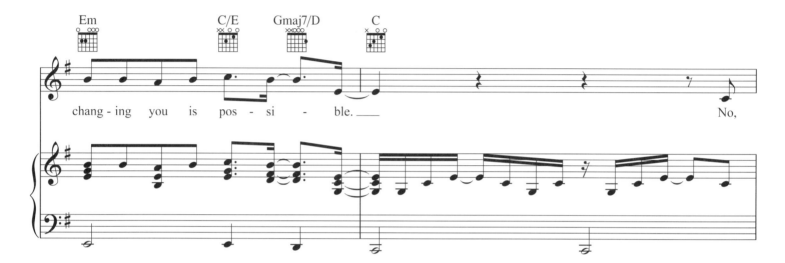

love is nev - er log - i - cal.

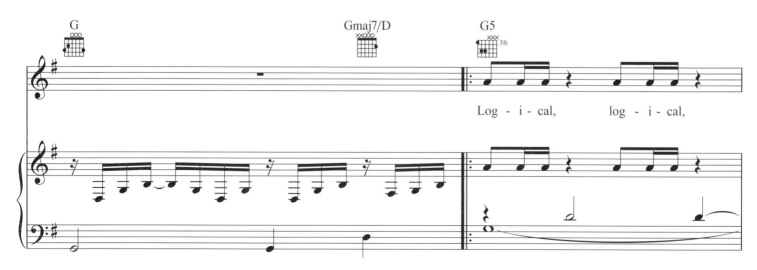

Log - i - cal, log - i - cal,

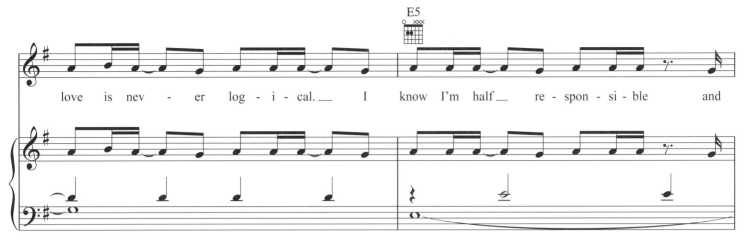

love is nev - er log - i - cal. ___ I know I'm half ___ re - spon - si - ble and

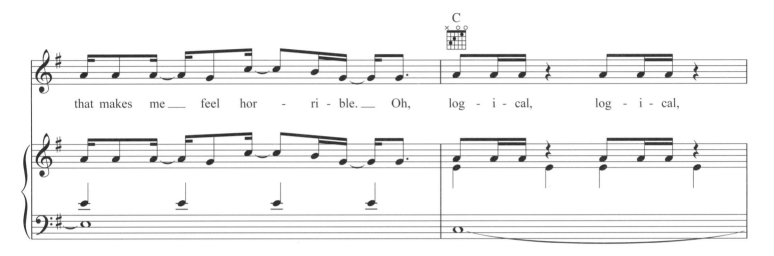

that makes me ___ feel hor - ri - ble. ___ Oh, log - i - cal, log - i - cal,

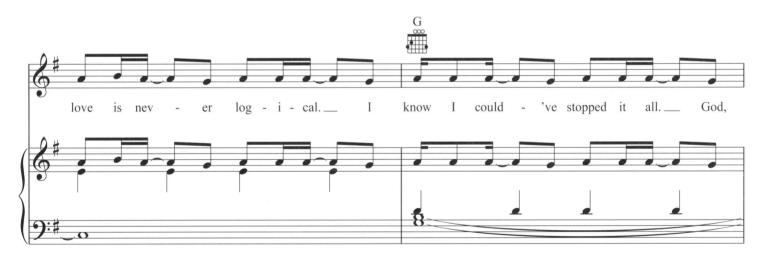

love is nev - er log - i - cal. ___ I know I could - 've stopped it all. ___ God,

1

why did - n't ___ I stop ___ it all? ___ Oh,

2

why did - n't ___ I stop ___ it all? ___

LOSE CONTROL

Words and Music by JATEN DIMSDALE,
MIKKY EKKO, JOSHUA COLEMAN, JULIAN BUNETTA
and MARCO ANTONIO RODRIGUEZ DIAZ JR.

no good at be-ing a-lone? Yeah, it's tak-ing a toll on me. Try-ing my best to keep from

tear-ing the skin off my bones. Don't you know? I lose con -

trol _____ when you're not next to me. I'm

fall-ing a - part right in front of you; can't you see? ___ I lose con -

with you I'm an ad-dict, and I need some re - lief, my skin and your teeth. Can't see the for - est through the

trees. Got me down on my knees. Dar - lin', please, oh. _____ I lose con -

trol _____ when you're not next to me. I'm

fall - ing a - part right in front of you; can't you see? ___ I lose con -

trol _____ when you're not next to me. Yeah, you're

break-ing my heart, ba - by. You make a mess of me. _____ Yeah. _____

Guitar solo

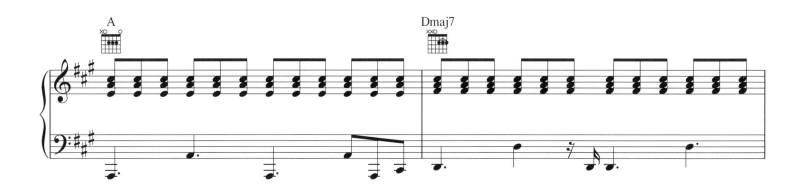

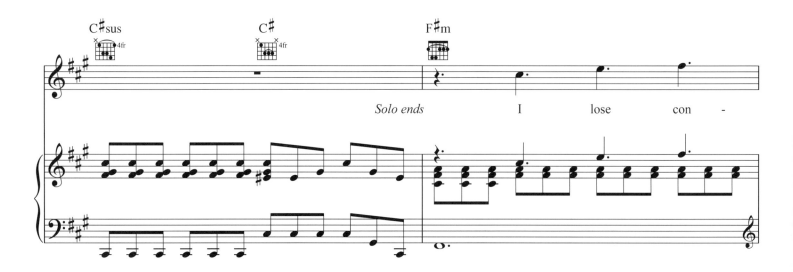

Solo ends I lose con -

trol _____ when you're not here with me. _____ I'm

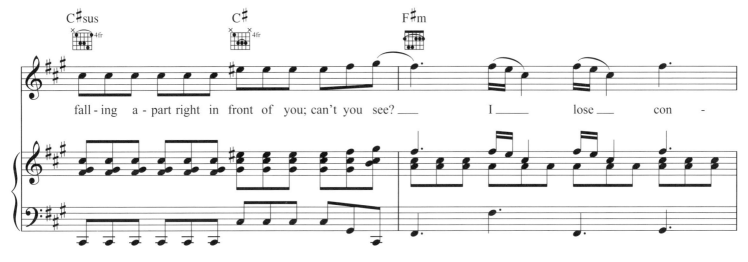

fall - ing a - part right in front of you; can't you see? ____ I ____ lose ____ con -

trol _____ when you're not here with me. Yeah, you're

break - ing my heart, ba - by. You make a mess of me. _____

THIS WISH

from WISH

Music by JULIA MICHAELS,
BENJAMIN RICE and JP SAXE
Lyrics by JULIA MICHAELS

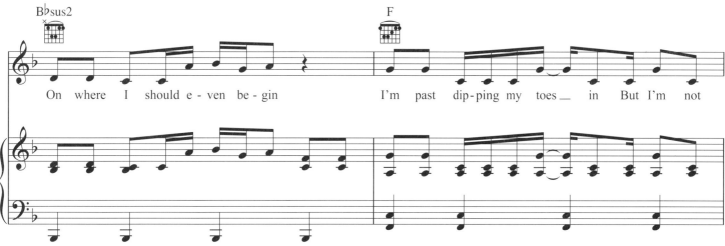

On where I should e-ven be-gin   I'm past dip-ping my toes __ in   But I'm not

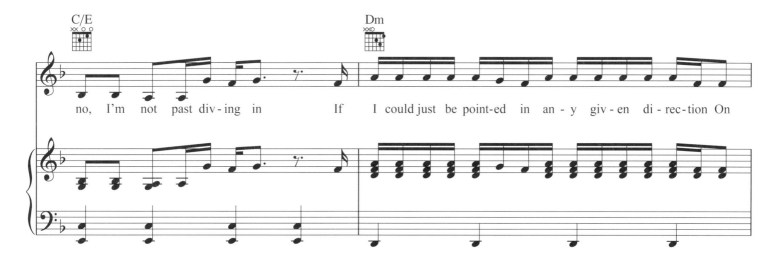

no, I'm not past div-ing in   If I could just be point-ed in an-y giv-en di-rec-tion   On

where to go __ and what to do   My legs are shak-ing but my __ head's held high   The

D.S. al Coda

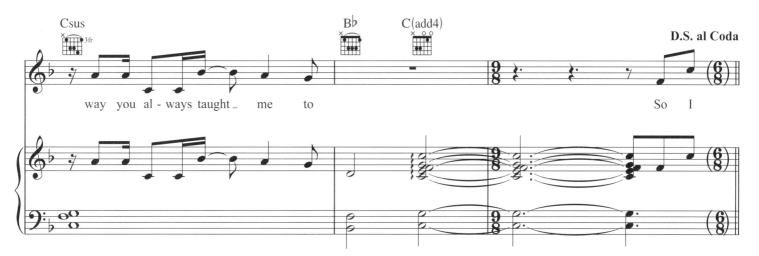

way you al-ways taught __ me to   So I

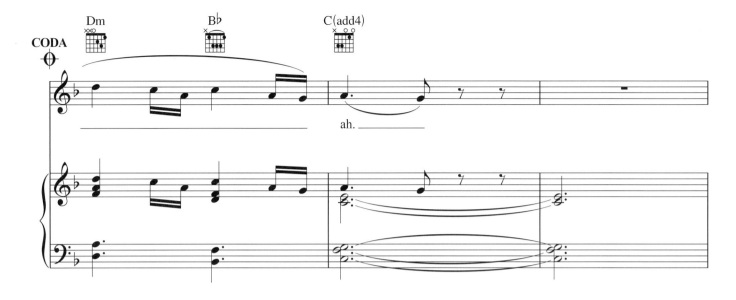

CODA

Dm   B♭   C(add4)

ah.

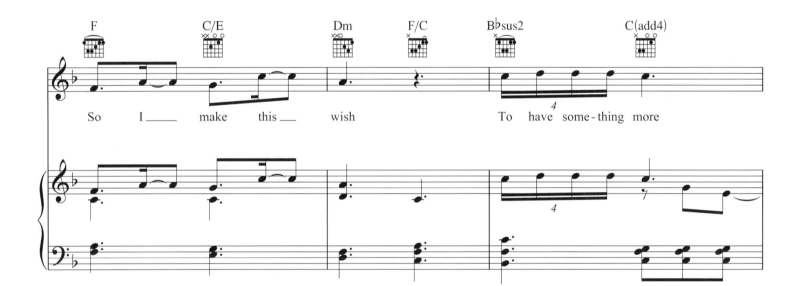

F   C/E   Dm   F/C   B♭sus2   C(add4)

So I ___ make this ___ wish   To have some-thing more

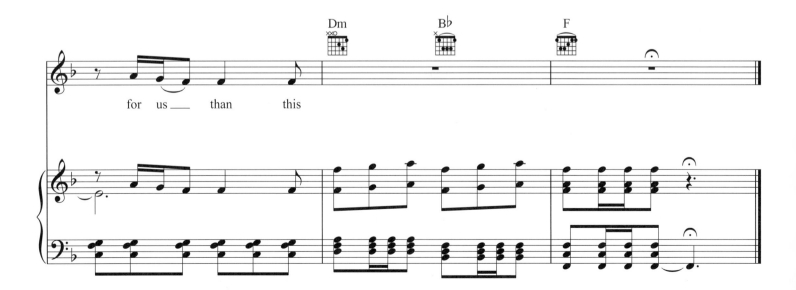

Dm   B♭   F

for us ___ than   this

NOW AND THEN

Words and Music by JOHN LENNON,
PAUL McCARTNEY, GEORGE HARRISON
and RICHARD STARKEY

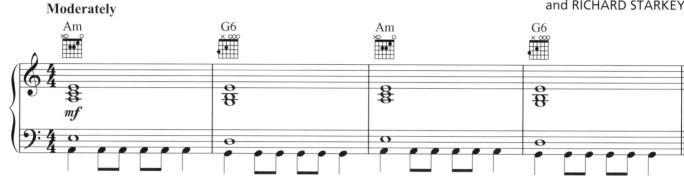

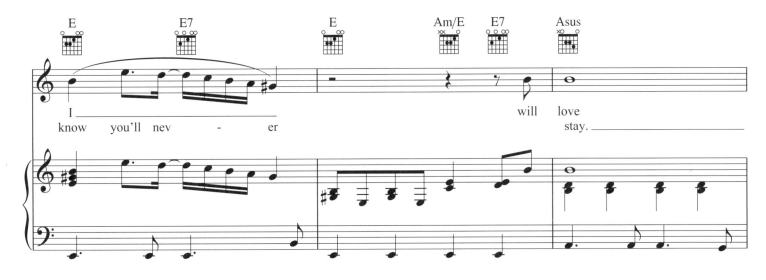

Oh, ___ now   and then ___   I want ___ you to be

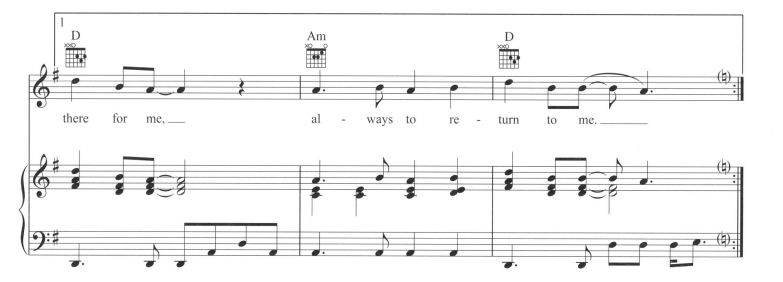

there for me, ___   al - ways to re - turn to me. ___

there for me. ___

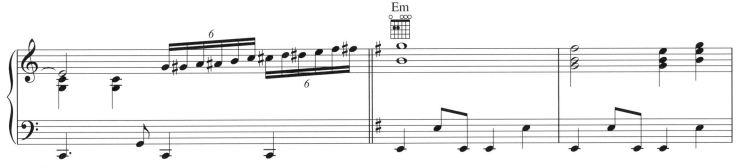

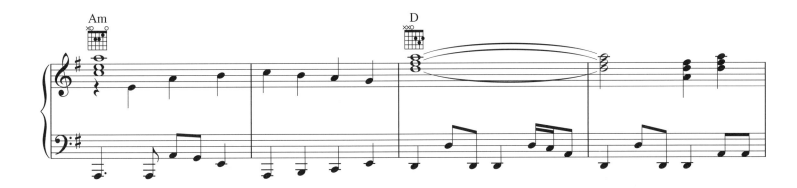

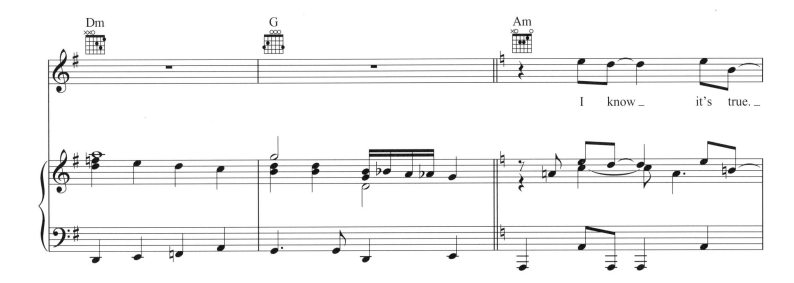

I know _ it's true. _

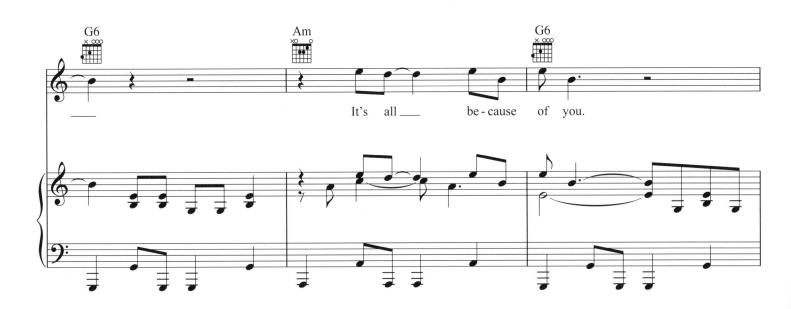

It's all ___ be-cause of you.

And if ___ I make it through, ___ it's all be - cause

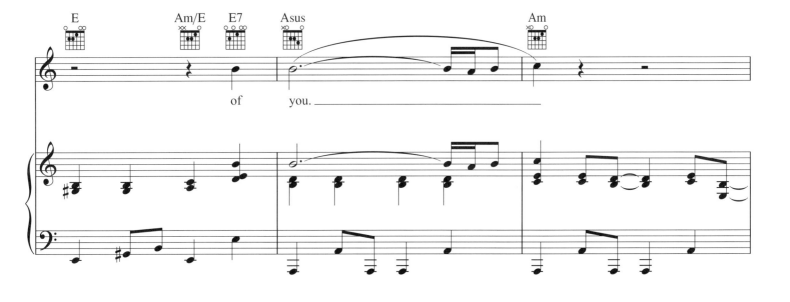

of you. _____

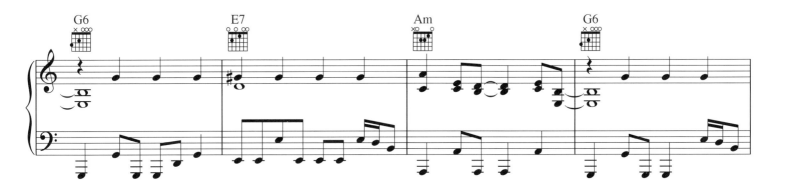

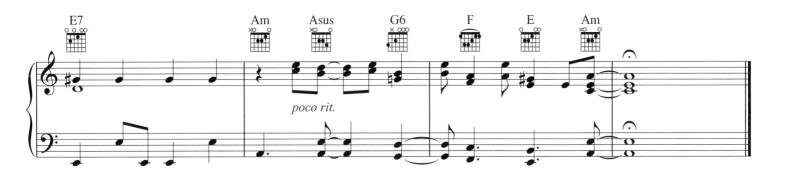

poco rit.

TURN THE LIGHTS BACK ON

Words and Music by BILLY JOEL,
FREDDY WEXLER, ARTHUR LAFRENTZ BACON
and WAYNE HECTOR

Moderately slow, in 2

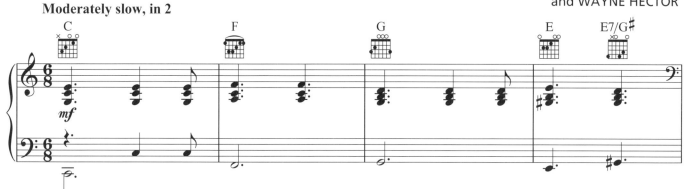

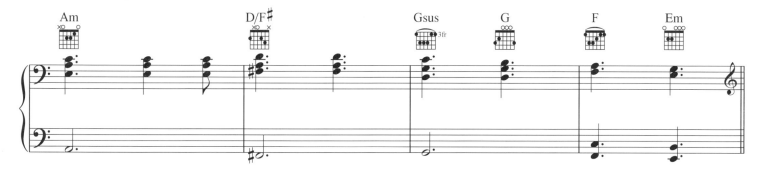

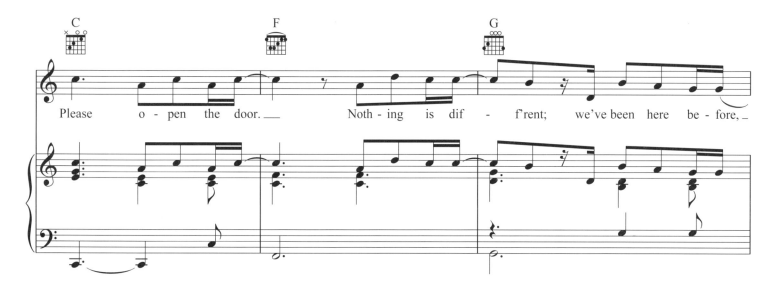

Please o-pen the door.___ Noth-ing is dif - f'rent; we've been here be - fore,___

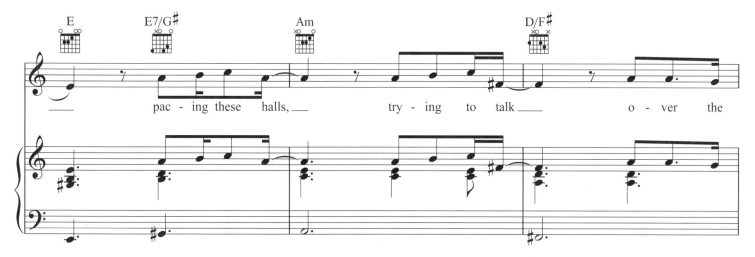

pac - ing these halls,___ try - ing to talk___ o - ver the

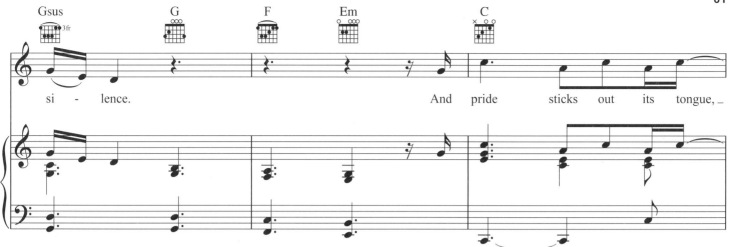

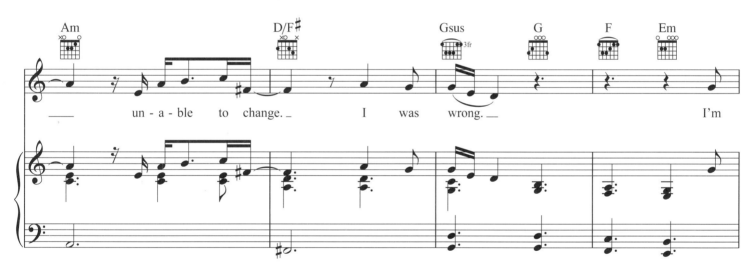

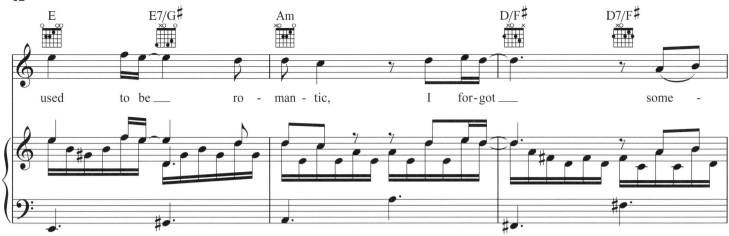

used to be ___ ro - man - tic, I for-got ___ some -

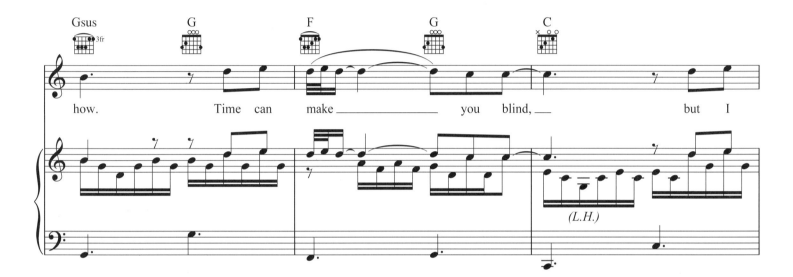

how. Time can make ___ you blind, ___ but I

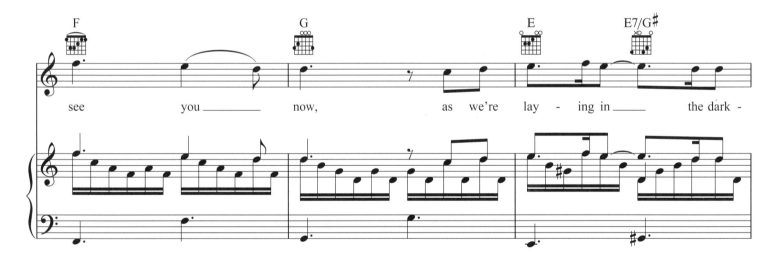

see you ___ now, as we're lay - ing in ___ the dark -

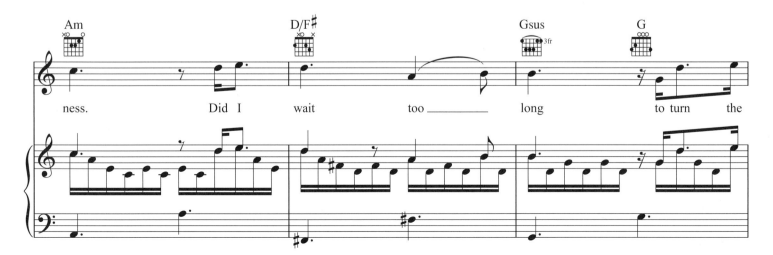

ness. Did I wait too ___ long to turn the

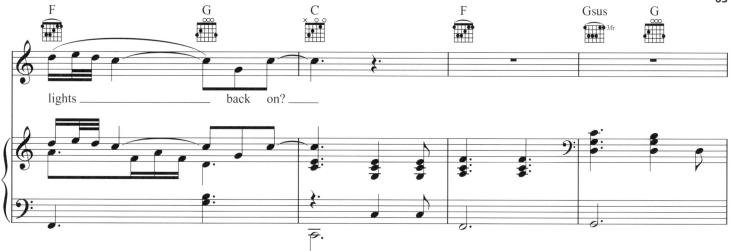

lights _____ back on? _____

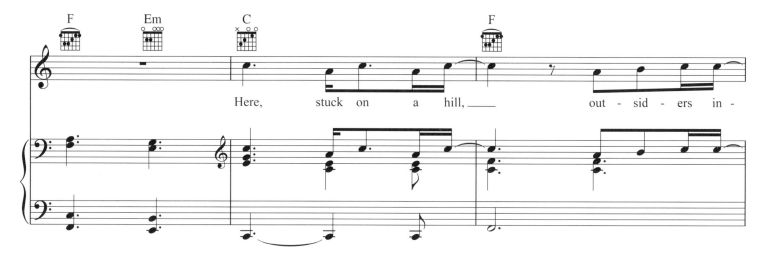

Here, stuck on a hill, ____ out - sid - ers in -

- side the home that we built. ___ The cold set - tles in. ____ It's been a long __

win - ter of in - dif - f'rence. And may - be you love ___ me, may - be you don't. _

May - be you'll learn ___ to, and may - be you won't. You've had e - nough, ___

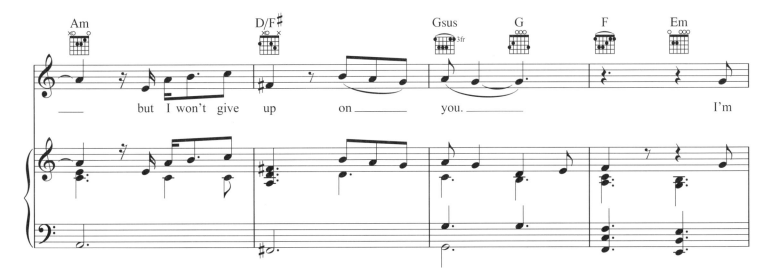

___ but I won't give up on ___ you. ___ I'm

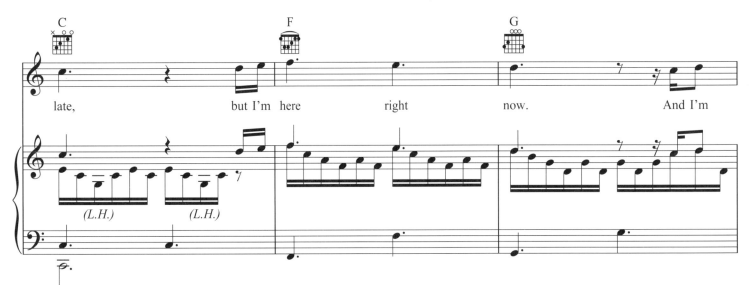

late, but I'm here right now. And I'm

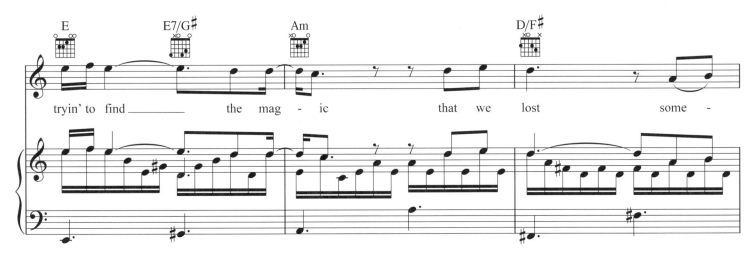

tryin' to find ___ the mag - ic that we lost some -

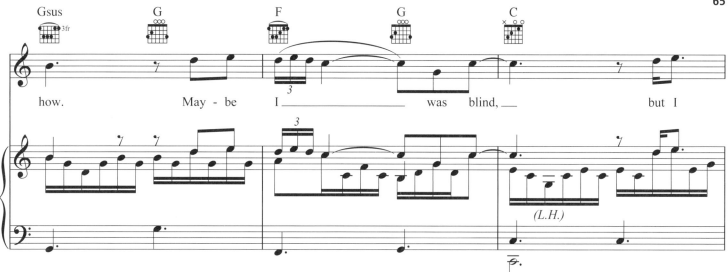

how. May - be I _____ was blind, ___ but I

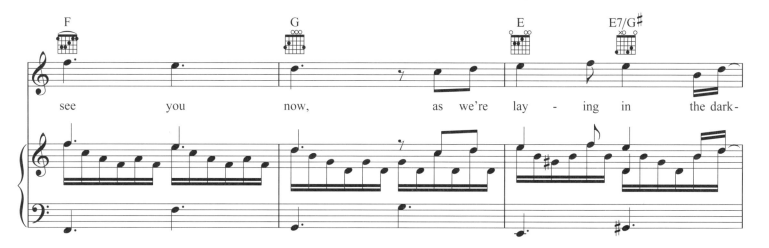

see you now, as we're lay - ing in the dark-

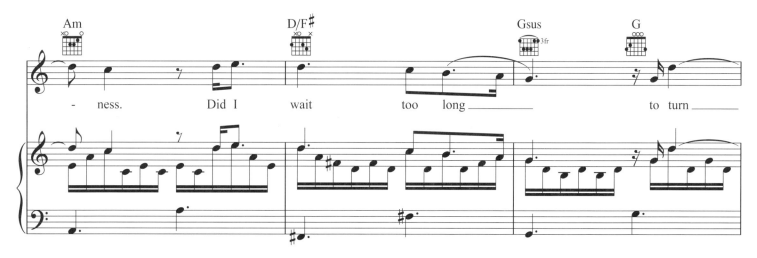

- ness. Did I wait too long _____ to turn _____

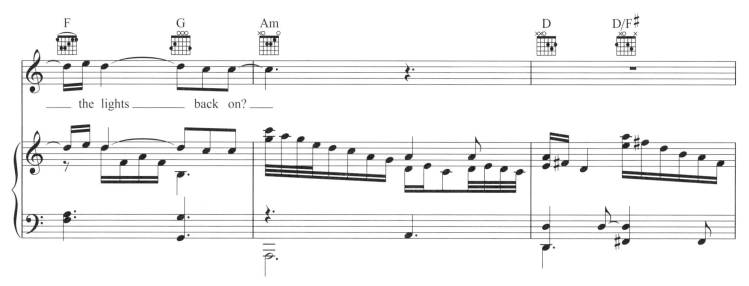

___ the lights _____ back on? ___

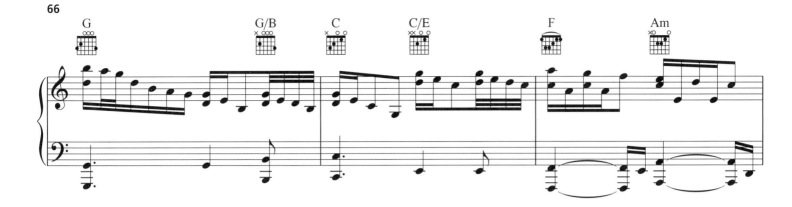

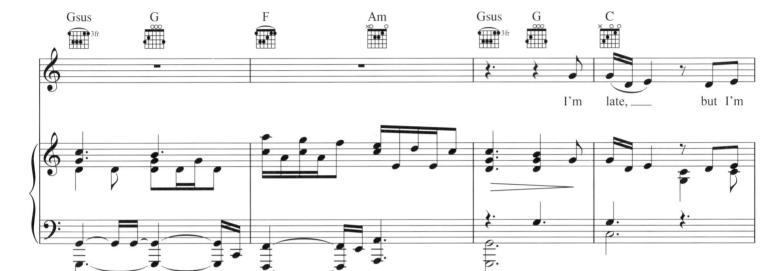

I'm late, ___ but I'm

here right now. _____ Is there still time for for-give-ness?

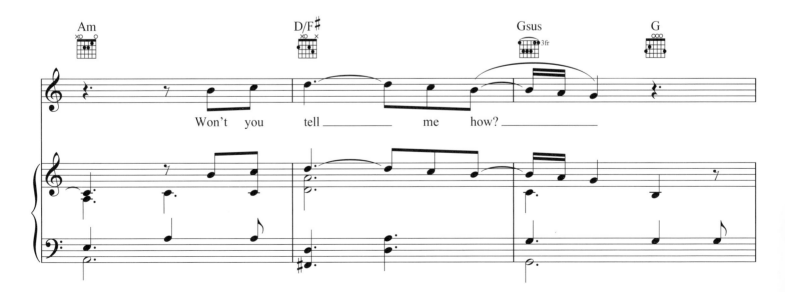

Won't you tell _____ me how? _____

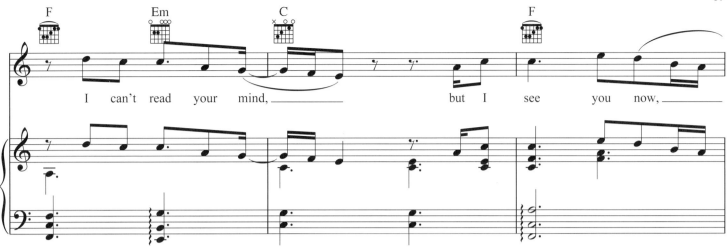

I can't read your mind, _____ but I see you now, _____

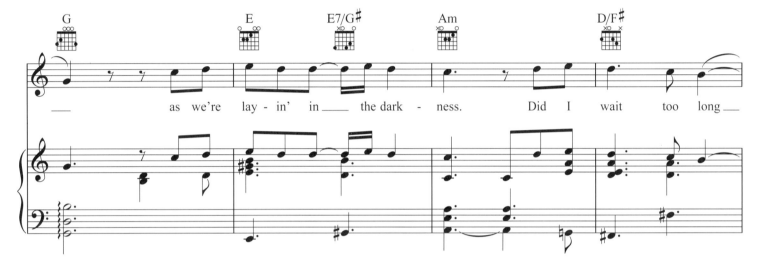

_____ as we're lay-in' in _____ the dark - ness. Did I wait too long _____

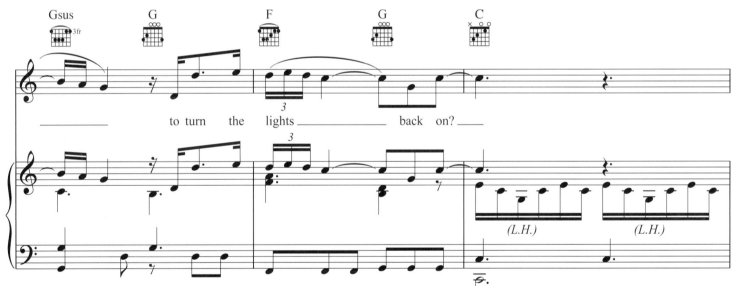

_____ to turn the lights _____ back on? _____

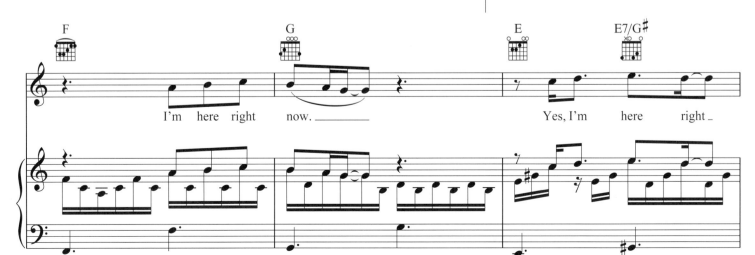

I'm here right now. _____ Yes, I'm here right _

now, _____ look-ing for for - give - ness. _____

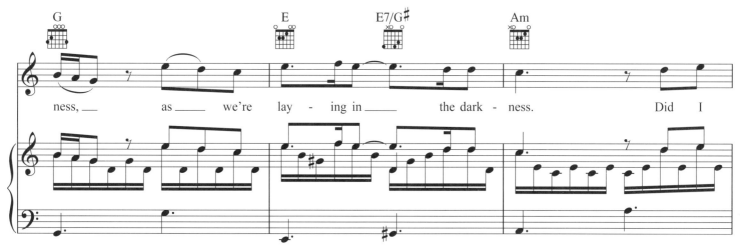

I can see as we're lay - ing in the dark -

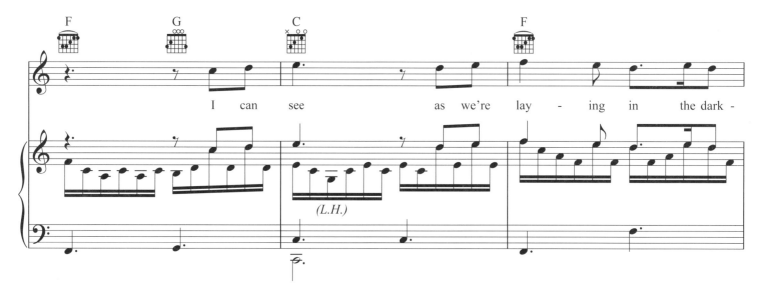

ness, ____ as ____ we're lay - ing in _____ the dark - ness. Did I

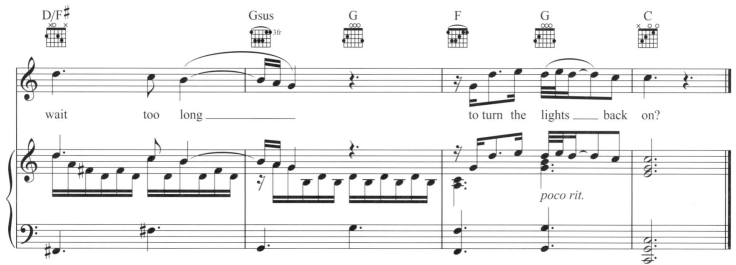

wait too long _____ to turn the lights ____ back on?

USED TO BE YOUNG

Words and Music by MILEY CYRUS,
GREGORY HEIN and MICHAEL POLLACK

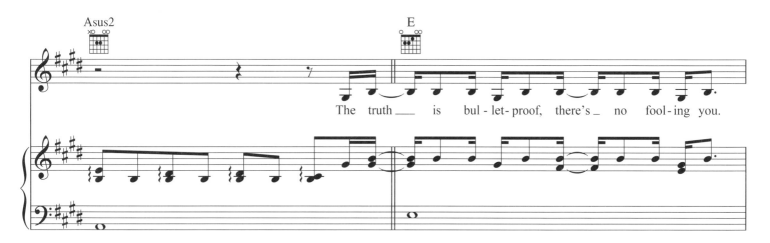

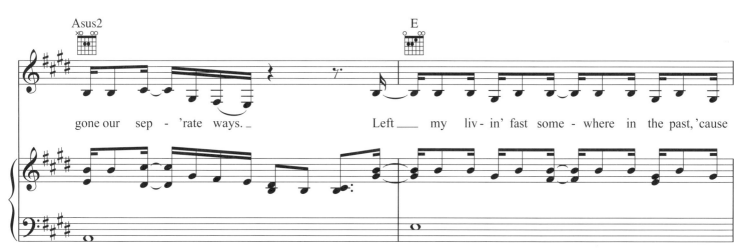

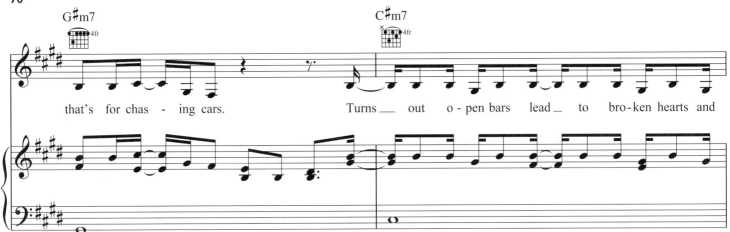

that's for chas - ing cars. Turns __ out o - pen bars lead __ to bro - ken hearts and

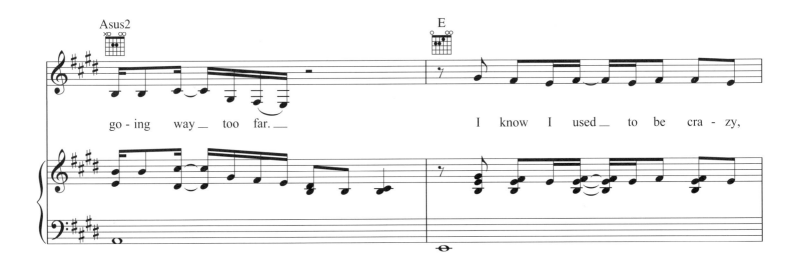

go - ing way __ too far. __ I know I used __ to be cra - zy,

I know I used __ to be fun. __ You say I used __ to be wild, __

I say I used __ to be young. You tell me time __ has done changed me.

That's fine, I've had __ a good run. I know I used __ to be cra - zy,

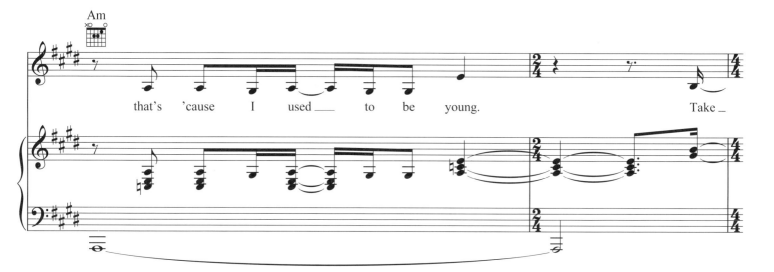

that's 'cause I used __ to be young. Take __

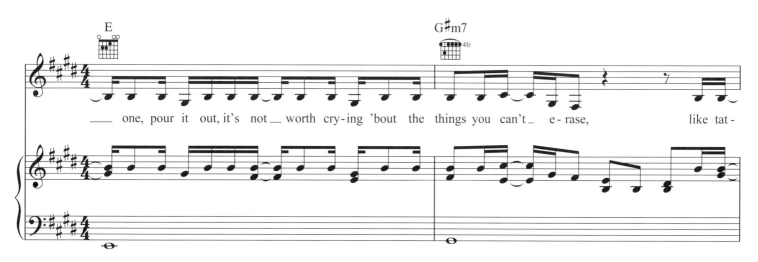

__ one, pour it out, it's not __ worth cry-ing 'bout the things you can't __ e - rase, like tat-

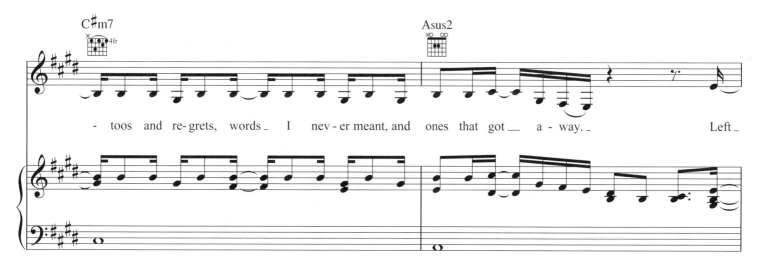

- toos and re - grets, words __ I nev - er meant, and ones that got __ a - way. __ Left __

You tell me time ___ has done changed me. That's fine, I've had ___ a good run.

I know I used ___ to be cra - zy, that's 'cause I used ___ to be young.

Oh. _____ Oh. _____

Oh, ____ oh, ____ oh, ____ oh. ____ Yeah. _

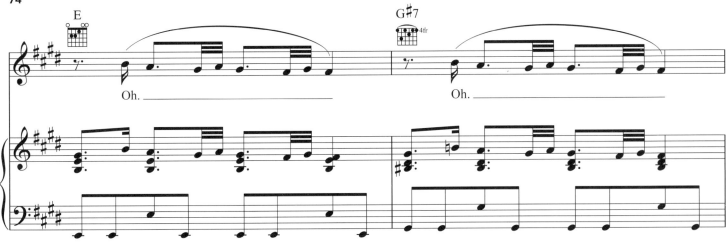

Oh. _____ Oh. _____

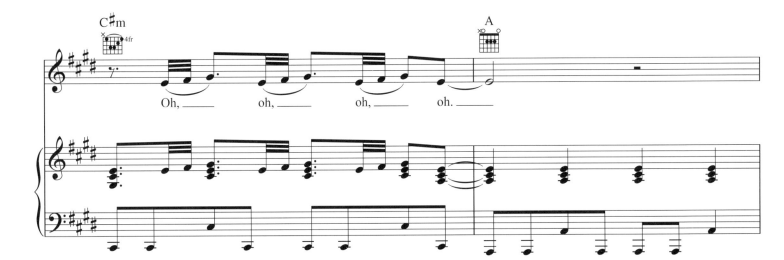

Oh, _____ oh, _____ oh, _____ oh. _____

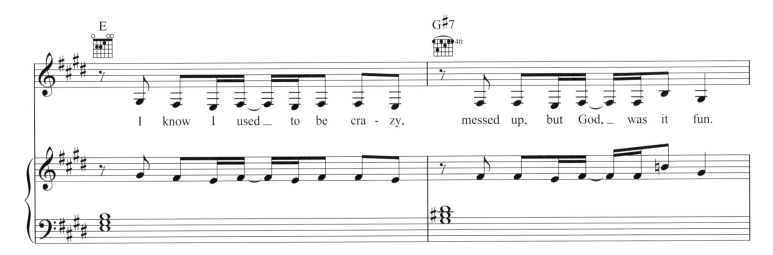

I know I used_ to be cra - zy, messed up, but God,_ was it fun.

I know I used_ to be wild, _ that's 'cause I used to be young. _

Those wast-ed nights__ are not wast-ed. I re-mem-ber__ ev-'ry one.

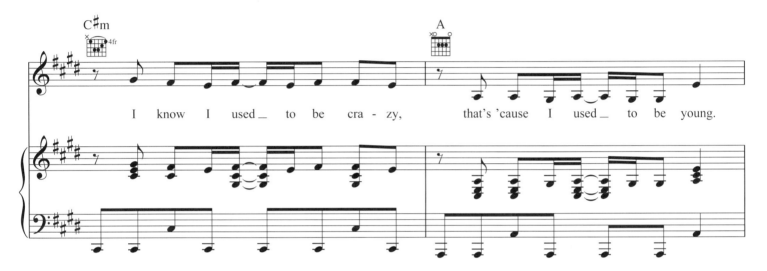

I know I used__ to be cra-zy, that's 'cause I used__ to be young.

You tell me time__ has done changed me. That's fine, I've had__ a good run.

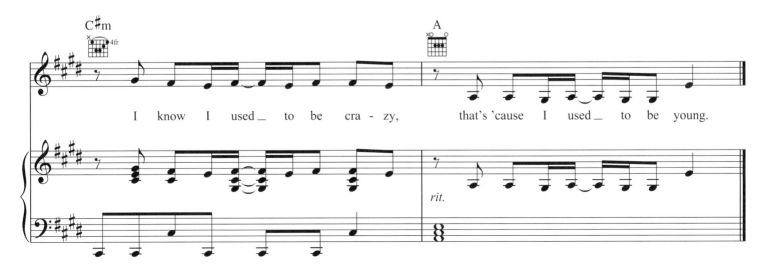

I know I used__ to be cra-zy, that's 'cause I used__ to be young.

rit.

WHAT WAS I MADE FOR?

from BARBIE

Words and Music by BILLIE EILISH O'CONNELL
and FINNEAS O'CONNELL

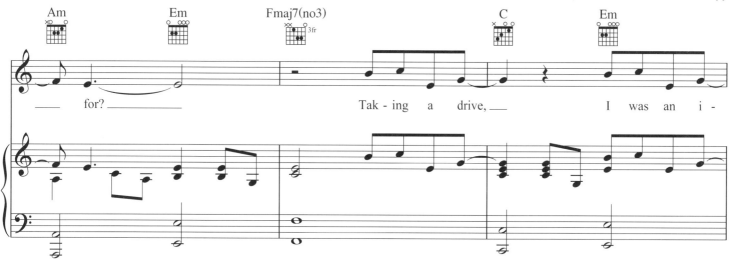

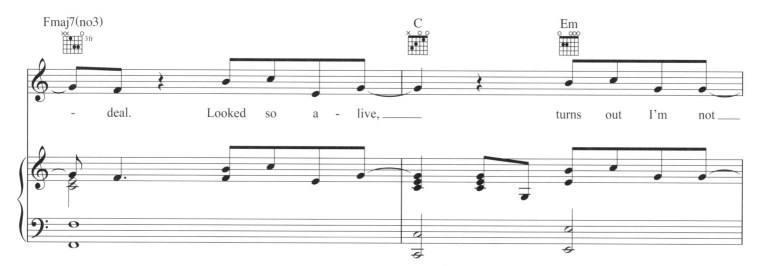

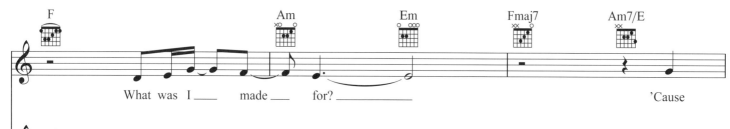

78

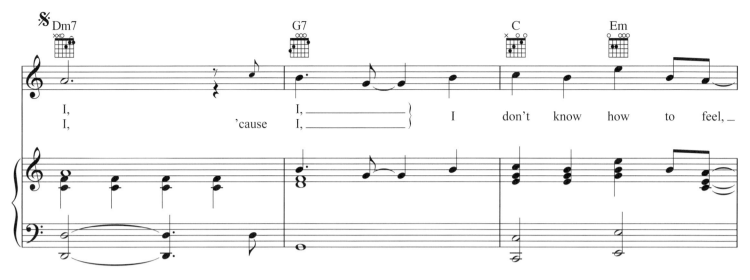

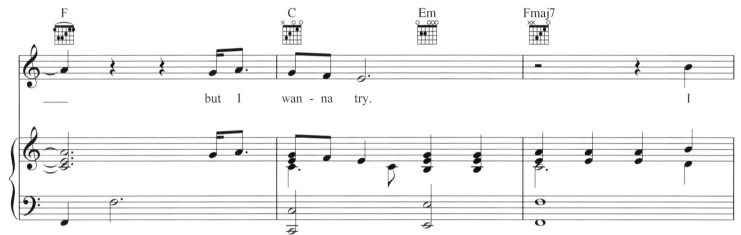

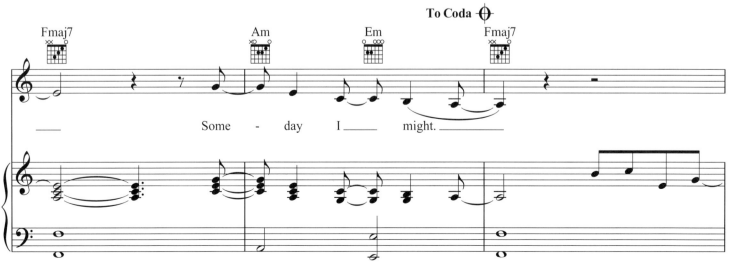

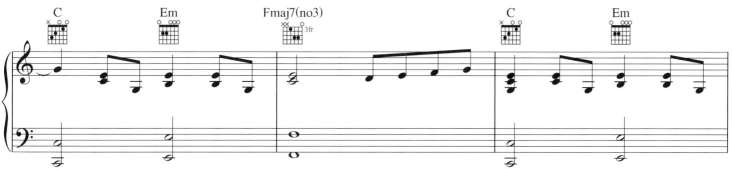

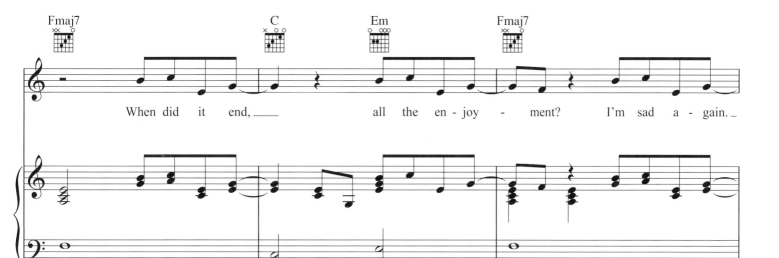

When did it end, _____ all the en - joy - ment? I'm sad a - gain. _____

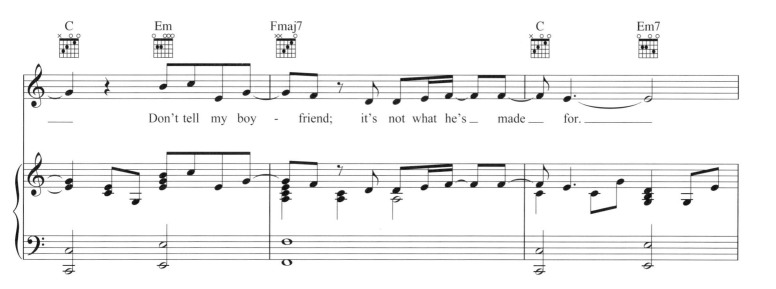

_____ Don't tell my boy - friend; it's not what he's _ made _ for. _____

D.S. al Coda

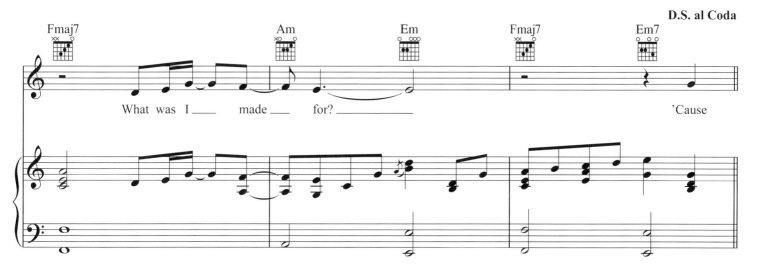

What was I _____ made _____ for? _____ 'Cause

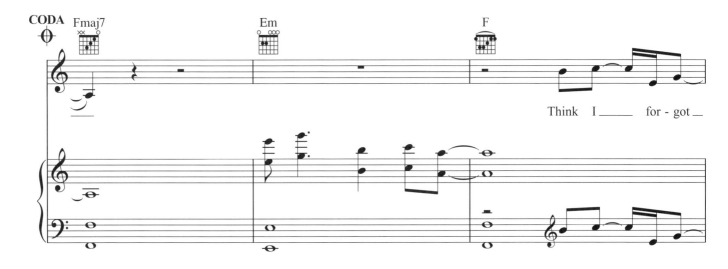

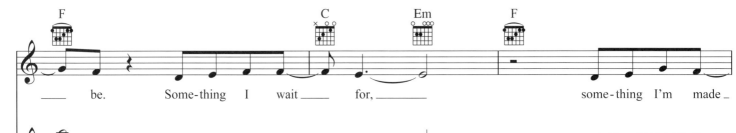

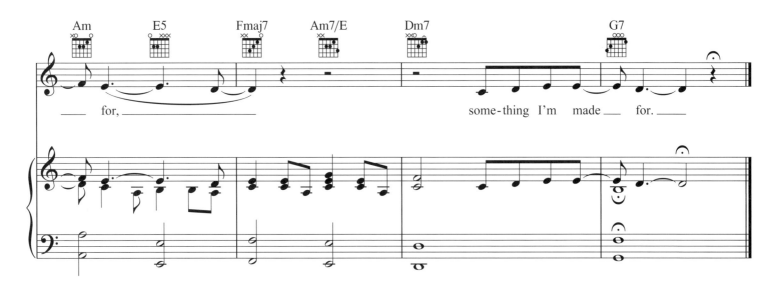